Text Copyright ©2014 Jeff Birch

All Rights Reserved

To my beautiful wife who sees in me the man I'm trying to be. Its been the highlight of my life building this life, our family together.

Thank you so much for everything you do.

To my wonderful friends who have stood with me though all these years. I hope that I have given you even 1/10th of what you have given me.

Thank you for everything.

To my Higher Power, thank you for giving me the grace of sobriety.

Thank you for driving me each day through your love, tolerance and forgiveness to be a better man, a better father, a better husband, a better friend, a better person.

For driving me to be more useful to the people around me today then I was yesterday.

Table of Contents

Chapter 1: I just wanted to be free...................4

Disclaimer:...13

Chapter 2: Leave yesterday behind................21

Chapter 3: My Story.....................................32

Chapter 4: What is a Wealth Wound?............54

Chapter 5: The Human Right to be Wealthy...64

Chapter 6: Income is built on Usefulness:......72

Chapter 7: More on being useful:

    The Altruistic Remainder......................84

Chapter 8: Income is built also on Control......89

Chapter 9: Do your Steps..............................96

Chapter 10: Your Future is built on what you do.

    Right Now. And only Right Now............102

Chapter 11: Responsibility Circles.................107

Chapter 12: Gather the Flock........................113

Chapter 13: Budgets and To Do lists..............119

Chapter 14: Putting it all together.................122

In closing,...130

Action Summaries..133

Chapter 1: I just wanted to be free.

The same way we have mental health and physical health, or emotional health and spiritual health, we also have health around material goods and finances. I'm calling wellbeing in this area "wealth health". Being wealth healthy is being financially and materially healthy.

In my experience, the same way we can become wounded in any of these areas of health, we can become wounded in our relationship to money. Just like I can have a wound in my arm or in my mind, I can have a wound in my money.

For me, ever since early on, I shied away from money, but really really liked having it.

That is, I shied away from talking about it, about facing my own deal. I never made as much as I thought I could. It was just money right? I told myself I wasn't as materialistic like those other people over there. I could live on less. So I never pushed myself to succeed. Not really. Instead I'd half ass it, or quit, or "decide to do something else".

When I tried working in financial sales for a major bank for a couple of months and was a failure, I felt like all these people I would try to talk to, that had money, knew something about the world I didn't. They were better than I was. They knew it and I knew it. I felt like I went begging every day when I went to work. I was groveling for their business- for their crumbs.

When I waited tables, I tried to make a game out of it, I played tricks with myself, flirting, giving away free food and drinks; I always was after that 20% tip. When I got less, for whatever reason, it hurt me. It really hurt. It would spin me out. My emotional reaction was too big for what the dollar value was.

I didn't open my mail. I got my first credit card when I was 18 and promptly blew the top off of my credit limit. I sort of intended to pay… sort of. But I didn't. With my first credit card came my first credit collections calls. Fuck them. "I'm not Jeff, you have the wrong number." I would tell them. "No, I don't know him, stop calling me." I defaulted on my student loans because I just didn't want to pay. I didn't make enough money to be able to pay that bill. So I let it go, never opened anything from them. Let them try to find me. "You can't get blood from a stone" I would say. They did. When they starting calling my family, I would tell story after story. When they began garnishing my wages and taking my tax refund checks, I was really mad.

I stole things from people. I stole from family, friends, strangers, from people I partied with. I sold the stuff I stole. I sold what I could, my blood, my body. I was doing medical research for a while as a research subject. I stole from whatever job I had. I tried leaving cities and moved out to the woods to get away from money, away from cable and phones and civilization, from status and competition. I paid overdraft fees, I paid late fees, I paid check cashing fees. I had account balances less than $20, less than $10. I couldn't get my money out of ATM's, my balances were so low. I was flagged on the banks systems that determine whether they'll allow you to open an account. I was refused bank accounts for years. "Fuck them" I'd say. I got by.

I borrowed money from people and if I could, either burned them with no payback or was really slow to pay. I've begged for spare change. I've paid in change, counting it out, ashamed. I would count out first quarters, then dimes, then nickels, then pennies. It's affected my religion and politics.

While all of this was happening, I still dreamed of having a yacht and a house with a big shower and heated floors and morning sun. I dreamed of having a home in the mountains, in the islands, of snowboarding, of sailing around the Mediterranean. I dreamed of having enough. Not too much, I thought, just enough to not be scrambling all the damn time. I wanted to be free.

For all the emotional and spiritual work I was doing, the truth is that deep inside I was jealous of people who had money. They had comfort. Their parents could do for them. They could do for themselves. I had a friend who began dating a woman with a trust fund from her family's business. I was so jealous. Jealous of her, jealous of him. I'm not proud of how I acted. I was wrong. They had everything I wanted. I wanted to *not* have to sell my soul to pay for things like electricity.

I wanted to be an artist, to travel, to read or to be discovered, something, anything, but be a fucking wage slave. A wage slave, giving up my life to make somebody else's numbers, I thought, of being terrified of what my boss thought about me, of having to kiss ass. No. I will not. Those people who had money seemed so at ease. They seemed so ok. It felt like they didn't even have real problems.

I felt lower-than. I felt less-than. I felt like I wasn't good enough. I felt angry, like it wasn't fair. I felt resentful. I felt like the system was rigged against me. All these rich people had advantages I didn't have. They knew people I didn't, had relationships I couldn't and I would never be part of their club. I wanted to burn it all down.

I felt entitled, you see, that since money was stupid and I was special, it should just come to me. I felt owing people made me less-than, like I was tricked. I remember just signing my student loan docs, never reading them, just doing what I had to for the next semester. I'd worry about that later, I thought.

I remember selling mortgages to people all over the country by phone. I remember being on the phone with them and setting up these deals. Paying off their car with credit lines from their houses. That work I liked. These people wanted something I had. I had loans. Those people I didn't feel less-than. Maybe a little. How was it that they could get a house and a car and I couldn't? But they weren't that different, I thought. I let them lie to me because I knew they were racing against the clock too. Just get them out of this jam or feed their greed. Turn that equity into vacations, into the good life. They weren't judging me. Maybe they were, but they were a lot like me.

Not like those other people, the ones that I'd dealt with at Bank of America. Those people made me so damn uncomfortable.

And when I did have money, I spent it. All of it. On whatever. I spent it on food, good times, taking people out, not working, paying whatever. Consuming. I'd tell myself I should save it, but I would just spend the savings last. I would set money aside and go eat out. I would set up a stash and blow through it on whatever.

I had no idea what the problem was – that I had a wealth wound.

I thought I had poor self-discipline. That I should just try harder. Do something different. Pray on it.

How does someone coming from this get to paying for our wedding and honeymoon in Hawaii, investments, a 700+ credit score, a 6 figure paycheck? Investors have joined me in my startup. How does of this happen to a guy like me? How is even more abundance coming? That's what this ebook is about.

I'm not perfect, I don't have to be. I just had to heal. You don't have to be perfect either. You can do it too. You can heal.

The secrets are in the 12steps, let me show you where.

---

*Note: Because wealth wealthy awkwardly rhymes, I'm going to use the word wealthy in its place some times. When I mean wealth healthy in this book I will say wealthy. When I say wealthy, I mean wealth healthy. Also, when I talk about wealth health I'm making the distinction between people who are materially healthy versus people who receive a lot of income.

Warren Buffet and Oprah are wealthy. Mike Tyson and MC Hammer were not.

Actions:

Write in your Wealth Journal: How has shying away from facing your relationship to money affected you?

Write in your Wealth Journal: What could your life look like if you became wealth healthy today?

Notes:

Disclaimer:

I've written this little book in the spirt of sharing- one person in recovery to another. You and I share this history of addiction and, together, we share this with millions of others. In my case it was alcohol. Yours could be alcohol also or sex, food, drugs, debt, prescriptions, gambling, or even relationships. In my case, my inability to beat my addiction by myself destroyed my life and health.

I understand some people will have a problem with this book. They will cite the AA tradition of "attraction rather than promotion". Let me answer some of those criticisms directly.

Firstly, this book is intended for people in Recovery who have experience with any of our 12step programs. The audience for this work is not the addict still suffering from their addiction, nor the general unaddicted population; rather it's us, fellow travelers on the road of recovery, members of our large 12 step fraternity. Even more specifically, this text is intended for those of us affiliated with a 12step recovery program with a long standing leading from their Higher Power to become healthy in our relationship with money, to become wealth healthy.

For some people, wealth health comes naturally. For me and for many others, it does not. This short book lays out the concepts and suggests activities that have worked for me, my sponsor, the guys we work with and the guys that work with them.

My personal root and the conceptual root of this book is the Big Book of Alcoholics Anonymous. The passages I quote are those of the second edition, which is in the public domain.

It's been my experience that I and those around me who work the program of recovery as laid out in the book *Alcoholics Anonymous'* first 164 pages live successful, happy, useful, sane lives, as they and their Higher Power work out the details. I've watched the people around them benefit also from their work in fellow 12 step groups, working the program, as the days of their self-inflicted pain and misery disappear.

Even if you are not explicitly familiar with the Big Book of Alcoholics Anonymous, the 12step program you do have experience with is, at its kernel, based in the concepts and plan of action laid out in its first 164 pages.

For each of the various 12step programs, the Big Book is conference approved literature. This is our root for our work. Since 1939, its promise to and actual delivery of recovery to millions of alcoholics and addicts is the promise contained within your 12step fellowship program. In my experience, it works, if you work it.

To the criticism that this book violates the tradition of maintaining "anonymity at the level of press, radio and TV" tradition, Jeff Birch is not my real name. I intentionally don't name specific people or institutions in this book to further anonymize who I am. I'm intentionally general in the telling of my story. Those that know me will recognize my story and some of those that are acquaintances of mine will recognize the things I say in here because they are my point of view, my experience.

To be clear, I may or may not be a member of any 12step program, <u>and in ALL cases, my views in no way represent Alcoholics Anonymous as a whole nor any of the myriad other helpful 12step based recovery programs</u>. The views, insights and comments shared within are entirely my own.

For our clarity, I think it timely to share with you here and now the long form of the Traditions that apply to this book. The source is www.AA.org and copied in their entirety below:

> Tradition 10. No A.A. group or member should ever, in such a way as to implicate A.A., express any opinion on outside controversial issues-particularly those of politics, alcohol reform, or sectarian religion. The Alcoholics Anonymous groups oppose no one. Concerning such matters they can express no views whatever.
>
> Tradition 11. Our relations with the general public should be characterized by personal anonymity. We think A.A. ought to avoid sensational advertising. Our names and pictures as A.A. members ought not be broadcast, filmed, or publicly printed. Our public relations should be guided by the principle of attraction rather than promotion. There is never need to praise ourselves. We feel it better to let our friends recommend us.
>
> Tradition 12. And finally, we of Alcoholics Anonymous believe that the principle of anonymity has an immense spiritual significance. It reminds us that we are to place principles before personalities; that we are actually to practice a genuine humility. This to the end that our great blessings may never spoil us; that we shall forever live in thankful contemplation of Him who presides over us all.

For those that object to charging for this book, I say that much like our concept that every meeting should be fully self-supporting, I believe that each recovery activity should be fully self-supporting, declining outside contributions. We do this to maintain authenticity.

Writing this text is a Recovery activity for me. I wish someone had written this ebook and gotten it in my hands 15 years ago. If they had, I would have been much farther down this path then I am now. This, to me, is an attempt to be helpful, to be of service. Charging for this valuable content makes that possible.

I'm also laying down a challenge. I maintain that doing all the activities in this book will bring you an awesomely high return on investment, literally a multiple of what you paid. If that's not the case, if you do each of the exercises in this course and don't experience significant improvement in your wealth health, I'll give you twice your money back. I want nothing more than for you to succeed, and I stand behind these lessons 200%.

For instance, imagine that the ideas, highlights, quotations, explanations and context in this book- like the principle of "constant thought of others and how you can help meet their needs" and the "Altruistic Remainder"-- support the seed in your heart to open a caring no-kill shelter three years earlier than you would have otherwise.

Let's say you've wanted to open this shelter for a couple of years. It was a dream of yours, unfulfilled. Let's say that as a result of this book, you begin to take action on what you believe your Higher Power's will for you. Let's say that without reading this book, you would have still gotten around to open the shelter, but three years later. Let's say that over those three years difference, the shelter opens and with help of others, it saves the lives of 253 cats and dogs. In addition, after covering your expenses, you make $600 over those three years. That $600 is more than you would have made if you had opened three years later.*

30:1, that means that for every single dollar you invest, you get $30 dollars of value. You could receive much more than that if I am able to charge less than $20 and or you make more than $600. I think the likelihood of you making more then $600 after you heal is an absolute. Try to find 30:1 in the world of Wall Street, real estate or even Vegas. This is a small example. This is the concept of Altruistic Remainder in action….the value you receive is larger than the price paid.

---

*To be technical, I'm intentionally ignoring the value you would receive in years four and onward because they compound on your activities in years 1-3 rather than starting from scratch. I want to make this demonstration of value conservative and easily defendable, rather than over selling pie-

in-the-sky effects, which are every bit as likely, though less believable at this point.

Based on the result of buying this book, at say $20, and putting its concepts into action, if you started your no-kill shelter three years earlier than you would have otherwise done, please know that you will have earned a return on investment for those three years of 30 dollars for every dollar you invested in this book. Additionally, and much, much more importantly, you would have reaped the incalculable value of saving the lives of those same 253 cats and dogs. Heartbreakingly, the converse is also true, if you had not been able to open the no-kill shelter for three years because these ideas and skills came to you later, most of these animals would not have had the opportunity to live.

Notes:

Chapter 2: Leave yesterday behind

We start here.

Leaving yesterday behind is something that we must do. We do this in order to have the creative capacity to be useful today. Being useful TODAY lays the foundation for Wealth Health tomorrow.

It is true that many of your ideas and actions in the past have generated loss and pain.

It is true that those decisions and actions were intended to have you reach your goals and become happier.

It is true that you were just trying to be happy as best as you knew how. Each of us are only trying to be happy the best way we know how. It is clear you failed.

It is really likely that you take the failures in the past to mean that you can't trust yourself. You may hopelessly believe that failure and pain are coming to you again, that acceptance is your only relief.

The past is not the future.

Let me say this again, the past is not the future.

It's not. Simply because something has happened in the past over and over again, simply its repeating over and over again does not prove that it will happen in the future.

How do you know this to be true?

Did you know that philosophers of science have known the past is not the future for hundreds of years? In the philosophy of science it's called the Problem of Induction. The problem, at the root, is that inductive reasoning, which is the formal name for this type of thinking, simply does not lead to knowledge of what is true.

The issue is a massive problem in the philosophy of science. As humans, we naturally and simply think this way. We are comfortable with it, it seems to make intuitive sense. The problem is that when you look at it closely, it's not sound, it just doesn't reliably lead to valid predictions. This is a nice summary of the problem by Wikipedia:

In inductive reasoning, one makes a series of observations and infers a new claim based on them. For instance, from a series of observations that a woman walks her dog by the market at 8am on Monday, it seems valid to infer that next Monday she will do the same, or that, in general, the woman walks her dog by the market every Monday. That next Monday the woman walks by the market merely adds to the series of observations, it does not prove she will walk by the market every Monday. First of all, it is not certain, regardless of the number of observations, that the woman always walks by the market at 8am on Monday. In fact, [David] Hume would even argue that we cannot claim it is "more probable", since this still requires the assumption that the past predicts the future. Second, the observations themselves do not establish the validity of inductive reasoning, except inductively.

These concepts were mind-blowing to me when I learned about this in class. I had taken it as "naturally" true that what had happened in the past was predictive of what would happen in the future. Specifically, that I would continue to get what I had always gotten. Further from the Stanford Encyclopedia of Philosophy:

> There is no comprehensive theory of sound induction, no set of agreed upon rules that license

good or sound inductive inference, nor is there a serious prospect of such a theory. Further, induction differs from deductive proof or demonstration (in first-order logic, at least) not only in induction's failure to truth (true premises may lead inductively to false conclusions) but also in failing of monotonicity: adding true premises to a sound induction may make it unsound.

With these philosophical concepts, we are lead to the only possible application of this knowledge: no matter what you have done in the past, no matter how many financial failures you have caused or been a part of, no matter how much of a train wreck you have been, they <u>DO NOT</u> mean that you will in the future continue to be a financial failure.

Our Past is not our Future.

The link you think you see, the link that seems so real, is, in fact, a mirage. The very style of thinking used to make your expectation of failure is not reliable. Great thinkers of philosophy and of science have known this for generations. Scientists just sort of work around it. In fact, this is why the very best science designs experiments.

In fact, the currently most accepted solution for this problem is called Falsifiability. Put forth by Karl

Popper in the 1930's. Falsifiability is the concept that when doing scientific investigation the only defendable track to arrive at Truth is to create hypotheses that are disprovable; since we cannot prove the affirmative. Please look it up if you are interested in knowing more about this controversy in the very conceptual foundation of scientific knowledge. It is a rich and interesting literature.

It's enough for us to know that therefore, for you and me, the expectation that you will continue to have poor Wealth Health because you have always had it in the past is patently false. By definition, this belief is, in fact, delusional. A delusion by definition is "a false belief that is based on an incorrect interpretation of reality". It's delusional because the evidence you use to support the expectation can't support the expectation.

Going forward, now that you know about the Problem of Induction, continuing to insist in holding on to this expectation makes your belief a delusional disorder. "A person with delusional disorder will firmly hold on to a false belief despite clear evidence to the contrary." So you know. There's no judgment to this, it's just learning. It's a common mistake. We all make it at some time.

A little surprising, huh? It's true, nonetheless.

ALL OF WHAT HAS HAPPENED IS NOW IN THE PAST.

You now are different from what you were. You are learning what we call the system of Wealth Health. You are getting the keys. You see that since your future isn't determined by your past, your future can only logically be built on what you do Right now, in this exact moment!

Let go of using the past to predict the future of your Wealth Health.

Don't be delusional.

The Big Book of Alcoholics Anonymous expresses this principle in what are called the Tenth step promises, the quote is: "we will no longer regret the past nor wish to shut the doors on it" and with a nod to our future discussion of usefulness to others "no matter how far down the scale we have gone, we will see how our experience will benefit others."

Now that you see that your past does not determine your future, know also that if you continue to do what you have always done, you will continue to get what you have always gotten-- NOT because of some inductive magic super-duper deterministic power; rather because you will regrow your misery fresh. Therefore our strategy is very simple—don't regrow the misery.

<u>Leave Yesterday behind</u>

<u>Don't regrow the misery.</u>

Actions:

Write in your Wealth Journal: List your regrets- Describe what happened, who it hurt, it what was your part in the regrets?

Share: Share your regrets list with another person.

Write in your Wealth Journal: Write about what it will feel like to make these same regrets again? Because very similar regrets will happen again if you do not change your behavior.

Write in your Wealth Journal: Name what was the best action you did today for your Wealth Health? What was it and how did it make you feel?

Say Thanks: Say thank you to your Higher Power for the power to have done the best thing you did that day for your Wealth Health.

Action: <u>Forgiveness Practice</u>

First step- Create a list of people you're mad at and/or have harmed you in some way.

Second step- Start at the top of the list and write about your part in the situation, what would you have done differently if you could do it over.

Third step- Reflect on the mistakes you have made

Fourth step- Understand that these people are the same as you; they are simply souls trying to be happy just like you. They're doing the best they can. And just like you, sometimes they misunderstand how to be happy.

Fifth step- Begin with yourself. Pray this Prayer for 90 days in a row: *"God thank you for the Grace to have made it this far. I know I've been doing the best I could with what I've known. Thank you that my old ways are no longer good enough. Please show me every day the way of patience, tolerance, kindliness and love for myself and for others. Please help me lay down those actions and feelings that no longer serve who you would have me be. Please show me every day who you would have me be and give me the strength to do your Will. Amen Thank you, Thank you, Thank you."*

Sixth step- Pray that everything good that you want for yourself comes to the person you are working on forgiving. As your heart softens, move on to the next person. Do this daily.

Say Thanks: At night, think about your favorite thing that happened that day and give thanks to your Higher Power for its happening.

Notes:

Chapter 3: My Story

I never wanted to drink. It was just me and my mom growing up in a row home in Pennsylvania. She was my mom and played the role of dad as best she could. I was also in Big Brothers/ Big Sisters and so had a positive male role model in my life from that relationship. As an aside, in many respects, that relationship with my Big Brother saved my life.

My Big Brother made time to see me every week throughout my entire childhood. He was like the dad I never had. He taught me how to shave. Big Brothers/Big Sisters is a quietly amazing organization. If you ever have a leading from your Higher Power to get involved some way, please do, you will never know what it means to us Little's. If any of you reading this are someway affiliated, Thank you. You mean more to us Little's then our words can ever express. Thank you, thank you, thank you.

Anyway, back to the story, my dad was a degenerate bum alcoholic, part of the endless procession of drunks that have always been since the invention of booze. He spare changed at the library for years and in his last years lived together with a blind, mentally ill woman off of her SSI. They had three children together, my youngest brothers and sisters. He had two more children by two different women as well, my older brother and oldest sister. I'm the second oldest.

My dad was an alcoholic, a general failure as a man and as a father for all of us. It was absolutely the last thing I ever wanted to be was anything like him. Recovery, for whatever reason was not in the cards for him. About ten years ago he died in somebody else's clothes. The last time I saw him he was lying dead in a cardboard box. That was not going to be me.

I had my first real drink when I was 14 or so. I was working as a wedding reception waiter helper and me and my best friend stole a bottle of tequila. Between him and me we killed the bottle. Growing up a row home and we had this little strip of grass between the sidewalk and the street. I threw up right in front of the house and grass didn't grow there for like a year. Nuts. I had an unbelievable hangover the next day, didn't really remember everything that had happened. Something about walking over cars and breaking windows (these were the days before car alarms were widespread). But I had relief.

I had relief from the pain in my chest, from this excruciating self-consciousness and judgment. It felt like there was a hole in the middle of my chest. It all just shut off that night, and I was free to just act. So that episode set the tone for the next years. My pattern was start drinking with others if they had access, by myself if they didn't, wander off, do some antisocial stuff and then lay low somewhere.

I didn't want to drink, but from the first drink, when I blacked out, that WAS what I wanted. So until I got sober, I drank every opportunity I could. Drunk for me was blacked out, if I could talk or remember, that was what I called tipsy. I remember once being so drunk that I couldn't see; or another time I alcoholically seized by myself under a bridge. I remember coming out of it by the drips of some sort of water on me and the smell of pigeon shit on my face, neck and chest. Very glamorous. I remember though, the drinking took away the hole in my chest. I couldn't feel it when I was hammered. I wasn't uncomfortable anymore. It is true I was malicious, angry, nasty, malignant predator when I was using, but I at least wasn't uncomfortable.

I first got sober when I was 19. I had been expelled from school for plagiarism. While drunk, I had hacked my roommate's computer, stolen his paper, and submitted parts of it as my own. The class was in my major and for my advisor. It was the last straw for the school I was at. They had been watching me for dealing drugs and alcohol out of my dorm room for awhile at that point. Drugs are a part of my story. Public safety officers had been pulling the fire alarm in my building disguised as "fire drills" in order to search my room.

When I was expelled I couldn't go home. I had been kicked out of my mom's house when I was 16. I would sneak onto campus at night and stay at my girlfriend's when I could. She would get me food. The other nights I just figured it out. I had an old car and a good sleeping bag so most nights I would find a safe place and curl up for a couple of hours. I had been going to meetings off and on for a couple of months throughout this. She was the one who took me to my first meeting.

I knew I belonged in AA. I knew it from my first meeting, when the speaker was talking about a hole in his chest. I had been to years of counselors and psychiatrists and never once had anyone mentioned the hole. OMFG, I was just like my father. I remember tearing up on the way home. I hated him and had sworn since I was little that I would not end up like him. AND HERE I WAS. I stayed drunk for the next month.

Later one night I got drunk again, same as always and may have done things while in a blackout that were bad. That relationship was over and I was arrested and charged with very serious crimes. I made bail because luckily, I had made a big score a couple of days before I was picked up and had the cash. Why I even had the option to make bail, I think the judge was in the Christmas spirit, there was some questions about the facts of the case, it was my first offense in New Jersey and my Public Defender and the judge seemed to have a thing. I'll always remember asking my mom for help with getting a lawyer and her mailing me pages she had ripped out of the yellow pages.

I spent Christmas that year at an alcathon because I didn't have anywhere else to go. I knew at that alcathon I would never drink again. I was drunk the next day.

A day or so before New Year's Eve day I violated my bond and left the state, going back to Philly. New Year's eve I was drunk again and in another blackout. I faintly remember pouring out a warm PBR around 4 in the morning, it was a quiet house wherever I was, everyone else had either gone to bed or passed out, and I was eating the last of their Crispix with raisins and brown sugar. They were that nasty soft stale that Crispix can get and the milk had really begun to turn. I remember that taste of souring milk, soggy cereal and warm beer. I remember burping it up, chewing on it and swallowing it back down. All acid and beer, spoilt milk, eyes watering, my throat burned. I just really wanted some bread. Fuck! What's wrong with these people?! I remember just being done. I remember thinking I'm fucked, it was all shit and this shitty shit wasn't going to help anything. That was my moment of clarity, a fleeting sense, a conviction, that things weren't going to change if I kept drinking. I was my father. I was a drunk. JUST. LIKE. HIM.

It was only a matter of time till a woman I had gotten pregnant would stop having abortions and I would have a kid. It was matter of time till I got locked up again, this time for something serious. I was an adult now. I didn't really run with guys. I was a loner, and if I was going to do time, it was gonna be hard time. I knew some guys inside, but we weren't good like that. My cousin was in, but what were the chances I would end up with him?

I was into stuff that when people got sent away for, they went for a long time. I didn't have any money. No connections. People had starting distancing themselves from me years ago. I had nothing nobody wanted. Growing up, it was always shut your mouth, keep quiet. I laughed when people started saying gangsters move in silence. Where I was from, you always moved like that. It was like that in the street and it was like that in the counselor's office. I wasn't trying to go away for anybody else, so I didn't run with guys like that. I knew that nobody was gonna do for me. It was a matter of time.

    I already knew I couldn't stop. Not really. I'd been trying. I had made any number of promises to myself, always changing my mind. I had tried different times in the day to start drinking, different situations and they always ended the same. Bad. They always ended with me passed out somewhere. I was never too picky about where I laid my head. I've come too in different places, with different people, with money I didn't start with, without the money I started with, with strangers, running from people I didn't know and didn't really know why, under bridges, in cemeteries, in woods, on back porches, in public toilets struggling to stand with dead legs, on trains, missing stops. It was terrible piecing together what happened in the days and nights before to find my phone or keys. Or getting those voice mails. I would always set out putting my stuff in the same pocket. Other people's porches was really common for me, because I like to move when I'm drunk, and I would just nod wherever I was when I got sleepy. I would nod anywhere as long as it was dry. I'd ride the trains and get kicked awake at the last stop. I would hop a fence and curl up- all this in a blackout.

I'm still like that, my wife teases me now, because she's learned that when I'm getting tired I just turn off. I will fall asleep wherever I am, even if it's on the floor in the hall. Just last month she woke me scared around three in the morning from the stairs. I had fallen asleep when I was reading some article real quick on my phone. I had left to walk the dog around 10, got back after walking the dog and just fell asleep never ending up making it to bed.

Anyway, back to the story, when I came too that day, I was on Regional Rail back to my Big Brother's house in Pennsylvania and the newspaper said it was the 2nd of January. I had some shit in my jacket that wasn't mine and somebody was going to be looking for it. I pawned it at some shop I didn't know and just laid low.

My first sobriety date was January 3rd 1993 but I didn't know it then. I went back to Jersey after a couple of days sick, detoxing, not telling my family down there what had been happening. They all thought I was going back to school. I shook off and on for a couple of weeks.

I had been going to a young people's meeting in north Jersey where I had made some people who would talk to me. My girlfriend was a member of the Program and I had linked into her group there. When I got back I found out she had told everyone she knew about what she thought I had done, what she accused me of. It was all icy stares, her friends would tell me to get the fuck out when they saw me coming in to meetings. I got jumped a couple of times and beat up pretty good. I didn't even fight back. I was just defeated and truthfully, what if I really had done these things…. didn't I deserve it all anyway?

Earlier that fall, on my own, I found this meeting with all these old people, people around 20years plus of continuous sobriety. Each of them older then I am now. No young people ever went to this meeting so those old folks didn't know who or what I was. I was the anonymous sufferer. They were always nice to me and that meeting had light sandwiches, cookies, coffee and tea! I didn't look or smell too great and I ate far too many sandwiches but they never told me to leave. I had asked a guy there to be my sponsor, and he agreed.

He was an old guy, with a USS Missouri hat, one of those vests with military patches, he was a no nonsense vet of something or other and took it all very seriously. He told me to call him every day.

So my sobriety began there. He was the only person who would talk to me in the rooms. He and that little meeting of old people. I had stopped going to other meetings because who was I gonna see? I had a court date in a couple of weeks, was looking at years in penitentiary. I was a homeless, penniless, dirty, angry kid with a lot of baggage.

But I got the change together to call him every day from this payphone that was in the basement of the train station, quiet and private. Roy would ask me if I brushed my teeth that day, if I had clean clothes on and if I prayed. I said no to one of those questions more often than I had wanted to. He walked me through the steps.

He recommended to me that I make an appointment to see the Dean that had expelled me. She agreed to see me and I let her know I took full responsibility for my actions and was sorry for doing what I did to my roommate and advisor and that I was getting sober and working in my recovery. I asked her for lenience, for a second chance and if she would support my reinstatement for one semester. My Sponsor vouched for me. I was allowed back on campus. She helped me with the administration so I could get my scholarships back on a conditional basis. Roy then started asking me if I made my bed. It was starting to work, so I tried to do what he thought best. I'd put my shoes underneath my bed and folded up my clothes.

Back on campus, however, my ex-girlfriend had told the community about what she accused me of. So in the eyes of many people there I was a rapist. There were even protests about having me on campus. I was still charged both on and off campus. She took heat for her stand and I can't ever repay her fully. I can only now be sober one day at a time and try to help guys that I come across.

My sponsor was just about the only person who would talk to me during those months on campus. That first semester back, I did 90+ meetings in 90 days and made the dean's list. I did nothing else but school and step work. Because of guidance I received from my sponsor and a lawyer friend he connected me to, we were able to present evidence to the grand jury that ultimately decided there was not sufficient evidence to indict me, all charges were dropped and the campus disciplinary committee ended up only censuring me.

I don't believe my sponsor ever liked me. Guys like him were on my 4th step. He looked different from me, wearing his mesh backed hat and vest with patches on them, USS Missouri, military patches. I never asked what his background was. I just didn't have the capacity to think of others in a way that didn't serve me. I couldn't see beyond me. I was in emergency mode. I wanted to drink every day. He would say all the time, "I am responsible for anyone anywhere reaches their hand out, I want the hand of AA to always be there and for that, I am responsible."

I think about him from time to time now, he died a few years ago. He made it, he died sober. There is no way I was ever able to repay him for his kindness and tolerance towards me. Even more then the Dean that did so much for me, I can only repay them their kindness by trying to pass it on and forward.

He also recommended that I go see a doctor that spring because of problems I was still having with my throat and stomach. I didn't have insurance so I just went to the emergency room, "let them figure it out" I thought. I found out then that my drinking had given me liver disease--alcoholic hepatitis.

For a couple of years, I had been drinking both denatured and absolute alcohol, whichever I could get, with orange juice. I used to call it my grownup screw driver. I would take my own booze wherever I went. I would only share if the lady was cute. And she would ALWAYS end up hammered. I had simply either bought what I needed at the drug stores or stole it.

I remember one winter breaking into the chem lab of a college not to far from where I was staying. I stole gallons of the stuff and used a sled to get the stuff into this basement I had gotten access to. I remember walking in the plowed roads to hide the sled tracks, slushy and slow. It was like my own pot of gold.

I had thought that I had found a loophole in the way this world worked. I thought that since the active ingredient in alcohol was ethanol, and that the label at CVS said ethanol, that it was the same stuff. I didn't know enough to know that they add poisons to industrial use ethanol to "de-nature" it. I drank it. Lots. I loved how fast it worked. I loved that feeling- when the drunk would come on like a wave. I was sober one minute and the next I couldn't walk. I ended up in the ER a couple of times, got my stomach pumped a couple of times when I took it too far. I would get ripped on a couple of dollars, thinking the whole time about how smart I was.

I worked the Program stayed sober for a couple of years. I turned 21 sober, I graduated from the school that had expelled me, sober. 2 days before my four year anniversary, at a New Year's Eve party with my cousin, I changed my mind and got drunk again. Over the previous months, I failed to maintain my spiritual activities. I had changed sponsors a couple of years earlier. I was putting off a couple of 9th step amends.

As soon as I had that stuff inside of me it was like the addiction never stopped progressing. I couldn't get high enough. I didn't talk to anyone, didn't care about anything or anybody, all I did was went back to the table for when it opened back up again after midnight that I could be first. I remember feeling annoyed right after midnight that all these people were kissing, standing around each other wishing Happy new year, IN. MY. WAY. I wanted that table to reopen NOW. That night, I couldn't get high enough, couldn't get drunk enough. I never blacked out. Nothing. All substances and thoughts. It was horrible.

For some reason, I was graced in that I didn't have to get loaded later that day or the next. New Year's eve that year was on a Wednesday night. That Friday, I went to the party celebrating my 4 years with my sober friends and had to announce that I had 48 hours. They didn't throw me out, they didn't judge me, they felt compassion for me, they simply didn't leave. We ate the cake and I remember, I didn't feel alone in a way that I'd never felt before.

I had always thought that a relapse would be this epic, dramatic struggle between the sobriety and the addiction inside of me. It wasn't. I simply changed my mind, snap, just like that. Whiskey in milk goes the story in the Big Book. That was true for me.

I haven't had to have a drink since. I celebrate my anniversary January 3rd each year, even though my true sobriety date is January 2nd, 1997. And I never spend New Year's Eve around booze anymore.

Where I'm at today is that I have a happy family life. I have more friends and deeper friendships then I have time to spend with them all. These friends are from around the country, from conferences, service and travel.

Some are still sober, some aren't. Some have done really well, some are still looking for answers.

My mom and I skype regularly, and it's nice. I have a healthy body. My liver, stomach, and esophagus have all healed. I have hundreds of positive professional connections. I have a sponsor and sponsor guys. I work a daily 10, 11 and 12. I live in a place that I love. I am excited about me and my family's future. I used to wish that I wouldn't wake up. I remember being bummed every single day for years when I opened my eyes and knowing I'd have to do another day.

I'm not ducking anyone on earth. I'm happy and have been this way for years. When I started this book, I was making a 6figure income from one of the top IT companies in the world. I've worked for four Fortune 500 companies, managing millions of dollars at each stop. I've managed groups and people. I was able to accomplish a dream of mine sober--I'm an Ivy League grad. I graduated Magna Cum Laude from the University of Pennsylvania. I've travelled. I've found a church I'm comfortable with and am active.

I and some friends have started an investment fund and business incubator. I, amazingly, have a credit score well above 700. This after I defaulted on my student loans- in sobriety. I've now left that bigtime job and I'm pursuing a dream of mine, I'm an entrepreneur. I'm fortunate to now be happily married with one son and another on the way. . We have a great dog, she's beautiful and very sweet. My family loves me, they aren't scared of me, they trust me; they give me the benefit of the doubt at every turn. (for those of us that have lost the benefit of the doubt in our relationships, you know how valuable that is) People respect what I say now.

I sponsor guys who sponsor guys and it is a bright spot of my life watching guys recover to help others. Each promise laid out in the Big Book has come true for me, sometimes multiple times on multiple levels. This past January I celebrated 17 years sober. Thank you, thank you, thank you.

A couple of words about my family background concerning material things, in case that matters to you.

I come from a family and background where seeking money was equal to "loving money" which, in turn, was the root of all evil. For those that grew up with Scripture you know this one: "for it is written that it is easier for a camel to pass through the eye of a needle for a rich man to enter heaven." I grew up in church, a couple of times a week, where showing off was a prideful act. Pride was a sin. A good Christian church, for the most part full of decent hardworking people, they did mission work, collected for those less fortunate, hosted food kitchens, cared about social justice, put their money where their mouths were, plain speak and dress.

The guys and girls in the neighborhood around me that made money when I was a kid and teen did things I wouldn't do to make that money. Some died. Some went away. Some got locked up. All hurt, I could see that. As I grew up I came across people who made money and they also did things I wouldn't to do, they were kiss ups, phonies.

When I was in the corporate environment, the competition, the covering up, the manipulations to maintain appearances, timelines and outcomes, the coldness, backstabbing, shadiness, were things that didn't align with me, my morals, and my spirit. It just wasn't the right environment for me.

For 25 years I've listened, read, bought tapes, watched TED talks, and interviewed wealthy people. I studied Tony Robbins, Robert Kawaski, biographies and autobiographies of Richard Branson, Ben Franklin, John D Rockefeller, Andrew Carnegie, Warren Buffet, Bill Gates, Alexander Hamilton, Martin Luther King, Big Momma Thorton, hundreds of people who've made an impact. I've read Thoreau, Schumpter, Huey Newton, Marx, Adam Smith, Lenin, Dostoevsky, George Fox, Ronda Byrne, Edward Cayce, Gabriel Garcia Marquez, bell hooks, Rumi, Ibn al Arabi, St Teresa, Zig Ziglar, St Francis of Assisi, Seneca, Dale Carnegie, Robert Greene, Tim Ferris. All in, I've read hundreds of books, around this subject. I went to grad school and studied economics. I studied psychology, I studied systems science, fitness, religions and spiritual systems, NLP, Cognitive therapy, Complexity, behavior modification, positive psychology, I took seminars, worked with Wealthy sponsors. I've had mentors and coaches. I've set up blog readers focused on developing abundance, trying to catch the latest thinking. I've read anything that I could get my hands on looking for the answers.

Each was useful in their own way, but none really hit the spot for me. The direction from my Higher Power was clear, I was to be wealthy. But how does that happen? I turned it over and didn't know what the next steps were. I am to be Wealth Healthy. I am to help provide for my family. For my sons, they will have a different experience then what I had. I am to be useful to others. I am to do Good and to do Well. That vicious cycle I grew up in ends with me. But what's next? As long as I was wounded, I was stuck.

What I'm offering is my own experience. This is what I did. This is what guys who work with me do to heal their own Wealth Wounds.

This book is about how to heal your wealth wounds, how to create wealth health and, most importantly, understanding how becoming wealth healthy aligns with and is fundamentally connected to our recovery from the incomprehensible demoralization of active addiction.

How to have abundance in your sober life? It's available to you.

We do this together.

Actions:

Write in your Wealth Health Journal-

What is your story?

What ideas of wealth were around you as a kid?

What was your parent's relationship to money?

What was your close family's relationships to money?

What was your neighborhood like?

Did someone close to you make a lot of money? How were they treated?

Was your family financially healthy or did they do the best they knew how?

What stories were told about wealth and money?

Notes:

Chapter 4: What is a Wealth Wound?

What's a wealth wound? Here's how to diagnose yourself.

Complete this sentence: *A rich person is: _____.*

If your answer contained a judgment, something with a negative emotional tone, or something that you don't like, you have a wealth wound. It's really that simple. Somebody is wounded in their relationship to wealth when they hold a negative emotional association with the idea of being rich, affluent, abundant…with being wealthy.

For me, I felt that wealthy people were stuck up, they weren't "real", they were fearful, they were judgmental, they were stiff, they worried about "appearances", shallow, they were unfairly lucky, they were only interested in making money, they were takers from "real" people, they were cunning and tricky, they were cold, they were phony. They kissed ass. They were different. I didn't want to be any of those things. I still don't.

The truth is that in all the ways that matter, wealthy people are no different than you and I. They are, like we are, just trying to be happy. They are trying to get by with what they know about the world. They are trying to be happy by following ways of being that they were taught, just like we are. It's just that what they know of the world may not be true, just like some of our beliefs are. Some of them could be thinking that they just "know" that the world is trying to take their stuff. They could "feel" insecure and threatened about that. And so they act in certain ways. I know that I've felt insecure about things and acted poorly out of those ideas. For instance, growing up my house was humble and not very inviting, so as a result, I never had anybody over. Kids in the neighborhood thought I was secret and distant. Maybe I was, but it was driven from shame, not pride.

I know that saying we are the same on all the ways that matter seems really kumbaya, but it's still true nonetheless. They ARE just like you and I. They have dreams and hopes, they love their kids, feel pain, they get dumped, they don't get the thing they really want, they care about stuff outside of themselves. They get scared. They get prideful, they like looking good to others. They like to enjoy themselves. They want to be safe. They get mad and get petty. They want to feel cared for and loved. They want to help the ones they love. In everything that matters we are the same- you and I, them and us. If you don't believe me, that is your wealth woundedness talking. The wound creates separation in your heart and in your mind.

Left untreated, these wounds cause a lifetime of financial frustration and lack.

We are taught by each other to envy, to strive for the "good" things, we revere the very rich, with little regard to their conduct and character. We are taught to admire material success, even at the expense of things we say are more important. I was counselled by my career coach to spend more time networking with the people outside of work, rather than spend the time with my son and wife. "To put in the time", he called it.

What happens is that these negative associations we carry in the form of wounds create an emotional ambivalence within the sufferer. A strong and irrepressible come-here-go-away feeling. We are familiar with this idea in relationships, but we can see it in our material health as well. That ambivalence, that mixed emotion always handicaps. In severe cases, the ambivalence creates financially self-destructive activities and a life time of economic insecurity and frustration.

That emotional ambivalence always blocks the wounded from executing on their long term goals by causing instability and internal conflict. The loss is three fold- first, it harms us now in the day-to-day by causing us to make unwise spending choices, by under earning and by procrastinating; second, it handicaps our future as a result of the procrastination and delay; and as you will later see, it harms the things you care about by taking from them a powerful ally.

Have you ever bought something you really couldn't afford? Ever do it more than once? If you've bought something that took you farther away from your financial goals, that is the ambivalence I'm talking about. Ever find yourself not really able to stick to a reasonable budget you laid out? Ambivalence. Never even made a budget? Ambivalence. Feel sick just thinking about budgets? Ambivalence. Ever find yourself unwilling to give up an expense and so had to juggle things? Ambivalence. Ever not be able to make a payment on debt cause you over spent on something fleeting? Ambivalence. That is our wealth wounds causing us pain.

Financial frustration? More than once? Across a couple of years? That's the self-sabotage borne of your wealth wound. That's the pain. That's the cost.

It is natural for us to seek abundance. One of life's greatest joys is to give to those we love. Financial lack prevents this. Financial lack prevents educational experiences from being had for our kids, families from travelling to be with each other, worldly experiences from being explored, adventures met, wishes to be made and filled, schools to be attended, medical treatments from being taken, dentist visits delayed, and causes to go unsupported. Financial lack causes us to take and keep jobs that destroy our spirit, that require corners to be cut, and sometimes even our morals being breached. Financial lack causes us to hurt people. Financial lack silences our voices, lessens our impact on the world.

When I was a kid, as you know, I was in Big Brothers/Big Sisters. Being a Little Brother saved my life in so many ways. I am so grateful for my Big Brother to have taken time to spend with me and be in my life. When I was around 8 I promised him that I would buy him his dream- a houseboat. I meant it at the time with everything I had. I still have not be able to make that promise, it still hurts. It hurts right now. I have a little shame around it.

Now, I am working on it and closer to it than ever before, maybe I'll be able to deliver it by 2016. But I carry that regret with me, because I desperately want to be able to give this to him- today, right now. That I've carried this for years is a consequence of my own wealth wounds. We all have things that we have been called to do for those we love and are prevented by financial lack. Who haven't you been able to visit? What gift have you not been able to give? What protection were you not able to provide?

Looking outward, in this world, during this time, what cause do you feel strongly about?

How do you feel when people you disagree with get an opportunity to have their voices heard? When they are heard better then you are?

How does it feel to not be able to compete in the arena of ideas? To not have your opinion, your viewpoint heard in that glossy type, with those powerful images and impactful slogans?

This is the frustration and uselessness caused by financial ill-health.

What do <u>you</u> care about? What things can you do very little about because you don't have the resources?

That loss, that impotence, that frustration is part of the price you are paying to your wealth wounds. The difference between what you are being called to do and what you are able to do today is called the Effectivity Gap. In Recovery we are called to close the Effectivity gap to zero; quoting from the book Alcoholics Anonymous pg. 77: "Our real goal is to be of maximum service to God and our Fellows."

Let me be very clear, wealth wounds generate ambivalence. That ambivalence is expressed as patterns of come-here-go-away, self-sabotage and extremes. We feel the ambivalence and self-sabotage as pain and frustration. As it takes from us our financial peace of mind, causes financial instability and material lack, reduces the impact and effectiveness of our love and care AND it robs from the things and causes we care about an ally and a powerful supporter. This is the devastation they cause.

Your wealth wounds cause pain, they will not go away on their own. They steal from you, cost you your dreams and your lay waste to your potential.

Actions:

Write in your Wealth Journal: Answer these questions in your journal:

What would you do if you had unlimited dollars?

What in this world would you experience?

Who would you take with you?

What would you do with your time?

What would you do for your kids? For your partner?

What would you do for your family? For your friends?

Who would you help? Why?

What would you make right?

What causes would you support?

What would you give to charity?

What would you have done if you had had unlimited dollars five years ago? Ten years?

Where would you and your family be right now? What would you have done already?

What would it feel like to be Wealth Healthy right now?

Notes:

Chapter 5: The Human Right to be Wealthy

When in your heart you have the calling to become financially whole, our next action is simply to open to it, to become willing to try new things, to open your mind to new ideas.

We decided early on that we were willing to go to any lengths for victory over our addiction. However the details of your heart presents, be it for usefulness for others, security for your loved ones, peace of mind for yourself, of being able to give more deeply to your loved ones, or to better support a leading from your heart, we have a spiritual obligation to pursue it. Whatever it might turn out to be.

In our third step we make a decision to turn our life and will over to our Higher Power as we understand it, praying only of knowledge of its will and the power to carry it out. If it is the will of your Higher Power that you are to become wealth healthy, it is a correct action, a sober action, an action for your Recovery to take all the essential steps towards healthy relationship with money.

To deny your Higher Power's will for you, either because of your wounds or your misunderstanding of things, is simply to move away from the Solution. Rejecting God's will because it is new and different or uncomfortable and scary is to move back toward destructive selfishness and active addiction. This simple fact our shared common recovery heritage makes clear. Let me quote at length a passage from the Alcoholics Anonymous, the central book of our shared Recovery path:

> It is easy to let up on the spiritual program of action and rest on our laurels. We are headed for trouble if we do, for alcohol is a subtle foe. We are not cured of alcoholism. What we really have is a daily reprieve contingent on the maintenance of our spiritual condition. Every day is a day when we must carry the vision of God's will into all or our activities. "How can I best serve thee-Thy will (not mine) be done." These are thoughts which must go with us constantly. We can exercise our will power along this line all we wish. It is the proper use of the will.
>
> Much has already been said about receiving strength, inspiration, and direction from Him who has all knowledge and power. If we have carefully followed directions, we have begun to sense the flow of His Spirit into us. To some extent we have become God-conscious. We have begun to develop this vital sixth sense. But we must go further and

that means more action. (Alcoholics Anonymous, pg 85)

Our highest happiness is found in giving to those we love; love finds its most natural and spontaneous expression in giving. Think about it, if you are a parent, think to your son or daughter's last birthday or big holiday. Think about how it feels to be able to give to someone you care about. To be able to spring for dinner, to buy that long desired item, to be able to support a cause you feel strongly about, to put a dollar in the basket, to help a loved one have an amazing experience, to be able to buy a cup of coffee for a guy who's still suffering, to give shelter and a safe place to someone, to do all of these things without having to short one of your bills, feels great!

Now think of the last time you wanted to give something to someone but you couldn't because you weren't wealth healthy enough? Maybe you just didn't have the money outright. Maybe you had the money, but you needed it to go somewhere else. How did that feel? How does it feel that it will happen again if things don't change in your life? We can almost always give time, attention and affection, often we want to give more.

The person who gives nothing lives a life of indescribable desolation. It sucks. I gave nothing to anyone for years, when I did give, I only did when I thought I would benefit more. I was living the sad, small, selfish, painful life of addiction. I was separate. Alone. It was cold and shitty.

It is perfectly right that you should desire to be wealthy, to be wealth healthy, to give and receive support. Imagine giving and for it not to affect your security or your bills; to not have to choose between the phone bill and helping others. All of us want that. In the same way it's perfectly natural to want and work toward physical health, emotional health, mental health, spiritual health. Who wants to be in a body with no energy, exhausted? Who wants to ache all the time, whose teeth hurt, who wants to look and feel like crap? Who wants to be so touchy that they end up screaming at people? Who wants to think people are stupid and always in their way? Who wants to be irritable, irritated and aggravated every day? Who wants to hear things that aren't there, or think things that aren't true? Who wants to feel desolate and cold, alone and forlorn, separate and damaged? Who wants any of that? We want health in all these areas. If you are a normal man or woman you cannot help doing so.

So it is with wealth health, being wealth healthy, with being wealthy. Who wants to feel that dread that the other shoe is about to drop, that fear of what would you do if your car breaks down today, that sense of loss that you can't do that thing for your kids, that scramble to come up with some idea to get the dollars for some bill, for the simple blankness of not knowing how you're going to do this thing that needs to get done, that pinch of shame when you think about having to borrow money? You can render to God and to the people around you no greater service than to make the most of yourself--to recover, and to become healthy in all areas of your life.

No person has the right to block or hinder someone else's becoming healthier. No person has the right to make another sicker. I believe the Right to Health is a human right.

I thought that wanting better for myself meant that I was ungrateful for what I had. Seeking to become healthier, I've learned, does not mean I am ungrateful. Wanting more and better for yourself and those around you does not make you ungrateful for what you have. Only by being ungrateful for what we have makes us ungrateful. Therefore, please, join me everyday in having a gratitude practice. Wanting to be healthier is, in fact, the expression of the desire to express yourself more fully, to be stronger, to have greater impact, to provide more safety and security, to have more fun.

The difference between your previous efforts and your efforts now in recovery, is that your path to becoming healthier is no longer about taking from others. Now it's by giving them value. By focusing on giving value and trying to increase the value you can give. By helping others have a better, easier, more productive, happier, more comfortable way, you become healthier. It's about no longer taking someone's slice, rather it is now about growing the pie by giving them more of what they want.

Actions:

Write in your Wealth Journal: <u>A Hundred</u>- A Hundred is a 100 item gratitude list.

It's to be done in the following format:

Thank you, thank you, thank you from the bottom of my heart for (the thing you are grateful for) because (reason you are grateful).

For example: Thank you, thank you, thank you for my son is healthy, because we would be so scared and I don't ever want him to suffer.**

**This list really gets tough after 40 or so items. Please push through and complete all 100. The benefit you receive is that at the end, when it's completed, you will be conscious for more things you are grateful for then you know right now. And that feels great!

Notes:

Chapter 6: Income is built on Usefulness:

Your income is built on your usefulness to others and your ability to control the method of creating the usefulness. In the NFL a player is paid so much because of his usefulness- usefulness to their employers, his Team and the League by drawing the attention of the audience towards the Team selling merchandise and to the advertisers that want to sell things as well. The more useful they are in drawing eyeballs, the more valuable they are to the Team and to advertisers.

Our income works the same way.

<u>Question</u>: If nobody needs what you do, why would anyone pay you to do it?

<u>Answer:</u> They don't and they won't.

For instance, I have a foosball talent. I'm naturally gifted, dominant even, on the table. Crazy right? Am I able to make a massive income from this skill? No, I'm not. There's some small tournaments around the country, but it's a very niche market. An ability to dominate on the foosball table is not useful to drive advertising on the scale that NFL player is able to. So I can't make NFL money playing foosball, it's not out there for me. It is no more complex than that.

Be Useful.

This is the central point. <u>Learn how to be useful to others.</u>

Then grow to be even more useful.

Specifically, in order to generate income, you must be useful in a way your customers will pay for.

Let's take a step back and understand the simple requirement "be useful" in the context of your recovery. In, Alcoholics Anonymous usefulness to others is a defining characteristic of health in Recovery. To make this point the book Alcoholics Anonymous uses a story of a farmer and his wife coming up from the cellar after a tornado, quoting pg 82:

"we feel a man is unthinking when he says sobriety is enough. He is like the farmer who came up out of his cyclone cellar to find his house ruined. To his wife, he remarked, "Don't see anything the matter here, Ma. Ain't it grand the wind stopped blowin'?"

What this means is that our addiction was the storm and simply having the wind and rain stop is not sufficient. They used the image of a farm house to make their point.

Back when they were more common, a farm house was a place of comfort, of shelter, of companionship. It was the center living space of the farm, of the family who worked it. It was the core, the place of celebrations of successes, of holidays, of sorrows shared. Of lives lived together. After the horrible destruction both to ourselves and the people around us wrought by active addiction, we are called to build, sometimes again, sometimes for the first time, the proverbial farmhouse.

This is what we are tasked to build by our Programs of Recovery. A place where people can come, find shelter and solace, safety and support. A place of use to others. A place where people can find comfort and shelter, companionship, safety and retreat.

Our shared central source makes explicit that our path of recovery is actually, in truth, a path toward usefulness to others: quoting pg 20- "Our very lives, as ex-problem drinkers, depend upon our constant thought of others and how we may help meet their needs."

Usefulness to others is the definition of character defect in steps 6 and 7. The 7th step prayer is:

> "My Creator, I am now willing that you should have all of me, good and bad. I pray that you now remove from me every single defect of character which stands in the way of <u>my usefulness to you and my fellows</u>. Grant me strength, as I go out from here to do your bidding. Amen" (*emphasis added*)

What is actually required is working to maximize my usefulness to my Higher Power and the people about me, quoting pg 77: "Our real goal is to fit ourselves to be of maximum service to God and the people about us." The message is clear: No person in recovery should be satisfied with a little usefulness. To be satisfied with a tent rather than a farmhouse after the wind stopped blowing is a "half-measure". Unfortunately, half measures avail us nothing.

The long term recovery we achieve and the happiness we experience as a result of this work is as a side effect of spiritual development expressed as our usefulness to others; quoting the tenth step commentary:

> This thought brings us to Step Ten, which suggests we continue to take personal inventory

and continue to set right any new mistakes as we go along. We vigorously commenced this way of living as we cleaned up the past. We have entered the world of the Spirit. *Our next function is to grow in understanding and effectiveness.* This is not an overnight matter. It should continue for our lifetime. Continue to watch for selfishness, dishonesty, resentment, and fear. When these crop up, we ask God at once to remove them. We discuss them with someone immediately and make amends quickly if we have harmed anyone. *Then we resolutely turn our thoughts to someone we can help*. Love and tolerance of others is our code. *(pg 84, italics added)*

Quoting Alcoholics Anonymous pg 130 to connect the dots:

> Those of us who have spent much time in the world of spiritual make-believe have eventually seen the childishness of it. This dream world has been replaced by a great sense of purpose, accompanied by a growing consciousness of the power of God in our lives. We have come to believe he would like us to keep our heads in the clouds with him, but that our feet ought to be firmly planted on earth. That is where our fellow travelers are, and where our work must be done. These are the realities for us. We have found nothing incompatible between a powerful spiritual experience and a life of sane and happy usefulness.

You can render no greater service to God and to those around you then by happily making the most of yourself, quoting page 102: "your job now is to be at the place where you may be of maximum helpfulness to others, so never hesitate to go anywhere if you can be helpful."

Do you want to know how to make more money?

Figure out how to be more useful.

Do it with your actions, say it with your lyrics, help your Team, show it with your brushstrokes, share it with your sounds, whatever your vehicle is, work at becoming more useful. Either extend the number of people you are useful to, or deepen the amount of use you are to others, either way, it's best to do both; it's really that simple.

Now please understand, it is not you that determines your usefulness, rather it is your customers, clients, fans and employers. They determine what is valuable to them and what is not. If you have difficulty with this concept, the action step to take here is to cultivate humility.

Discard the old tale that God wants you to sacrifice yourself and that you can curry favor by doing so. By sacrifice I mean in this context, burning yourself down to nothingness. That is not how our recovery is laid out. You simply cannot be useful to others if you are burnt out, without a capacity to help.

If you are an emotionally, physically, materially broke wreck, but nice to others, you are neither being of maximum service to God and others nor are you understanding your Responsibility Circles. Our bottom line metric in recovery is not consecutive days without active addiction, rather it is our usefulness to God and the people about us. If you helped one person yesterday, try to help two today. To quote pg 132:

> We have been speaking to you of serious, sometimes tragic things. We have been dealing with alcohol in its worst aspects. But we aren't a glum lot. If newcomers could see no joy or fun in our existence, they wouldn't want it. We absolutely insist on enjoying life. We try not to indulge in cynicism over the state of the nations, nor do we carry the world's troubles on our shoulders. When we see a man sinking into the mire that is alcoholism, we give him first aid and place what we have at his disposal. For his sake, we do recount and almost relive the horrors of our past. But those of us who have tried to shoulder the entire burden and trouble of others find we are soon overcome by them.

So we think cheerfulness and laughter make for usefulness. Outsiders are sometimes shocked when we burst into merriment over a seemingly tragic experience out of the past. But why shouldn't we laugh? We have recovered, and have been given the power to help others.

Everybody knows that those in bad health, and those who seldom play, do not laugh much. So let each family play together or separately, as much as their circumstances warrant. We are sure God wants us to be happy, joyous and free.

Actions:

Question: Ask your friends for ideas on how you can be more useful to your employers, your clients, your fans, your colleagues and your customers. Write their answers in your Wealth Journal. Your goal is to get a list of 50 separate ideas in your journal. If anyone repeats an idea, really try to figure out how you could make it happen.

Write in your Wealth Journal: List one thing for each of ten different people that you could do for them that they would find useful or valuable. Things that they would like and appreciate.

Write in your Wealth Journal: Write about how you could make each of those actions better for each of the 10 people. Possible examples are: by doing the action right now, doing it in a friendlier manner, or by reducing their costs.

Action: Do one of those actions <u>right now</u> for one of those 10 people.

Action and List: Go through your list of friends on Facebook and list one thing for each friend that would help them feel better, meet a goal, or meet someone that could be a useful connection for them. If you don't know what would help them, ask them now.

Action: Do one useful thing each day for each of your friends, including your Facebook friends, starting first with those that you see most.

Action: Each day do three anonymous good, useful, kind and compassionate deeds. Don't break the chain.

Action: Count the number of nice, kind, helpful, useful things you do for somebody else that you didn't feel like doing. Share that number with a friend or a group of friends every day.

Action: Tell a friend about the benefits you've experienced from these practices.

Action: Tell a friend about information that you've found useful, which would be useful to them.

Action: Tell a friend about this book and where they could buy it, tell them about the idea of Altruistic Remainders (More about Altruistic Reminders in the next chapter).

Action: Make an introduction between two of your contacts that would be useful to at least one of them. Make it warm and inviting.

Notes:

Chapter 7: More on being useful: The Altruistic Remainder.

So I understand usefulness. What about altruism? There is this line in the chapter Doctors Opinion, in Alcoholics Anonymous, Dr. Silkworth writes: "The solution lies in the altruistic and spiritual planes." Now what do we do about a thing like that? Does that really mean we're supposed to be super useful for no pay? My wound says I do.

My wounded way of thinking is wrong. Being useful is how you generate income. Be more useful, make more money. Give away some of that usefulness, BUT NOT ALL.

The concept is called the Altruistic Remainder.

If you provide something worth a dollar to someone, and you charge them 50 cents, the remaining 50cents of value is an Altruistic Remainder. The Altruistic Remainder is the difference between the total value to someone for what you provide and the price you charge. If the total value to them is greater than the price you charge, the difference is a value you are giving away for free, hence its name, Altruistic Remainder.

The converse is true as well, if you charge more than the value you provide, that difference is vampiric, named the Vampiric Remainder. Our path to recovery along the plane of altruism is in increasing our Altruistic Remainders in all the spheres of our lives.

If you have a customer and they have a problem, solving the problem for them is useful, and if you do it quickly and efficiently, with graciousness and kindness you increase the Altruistic Remainder. Makes sense?

If you PREVENT a problem from occurring for your customer- that is value you didn't charge for—that value is entirely Altruistic.

To be clear, delivering value that you do not charge for is an altruistic action. Altruistic action is commonly thought of as volunteering or giving away something useful at zero cost, but Altruistic action is not bound by that extreme restraint. It is true that giving way things at zero cost like by donating or volunteering, maximize the Altruistic Remainders but they do not determine the presence of Altruism.

By increasing the amount of Altruism in your everyday interactions, we develop along the spiritual and altruistic planes just as Dr. Silkworth says is necessary for our recovery.

The take away is: Give more where ever you can.

Actions:

Write in your Journal: Brainstorm how you could add value, even very simple value to those around you at work. Or school. Or in the car, all those place you find yourself. Try a couple of them this week.

Notes:

Chapter 8: Income is built also on Control

This is a fun one. The usefulness concept is clear. Be useful in ways people value. Let me take a minute to explain to explain the other leg of income generation: Control of the useful thing. Control of a useful thing is either through owning it outright or is given on behalf of the owners.

An athlete owns his or her athletic performance. The artist owns her art. A business owner owns the business. A homeowner owns the house. The general manager of a factory controls that factory. The general manager doesn't own it, but she calls the shots of what happens there and is responsible for its general performance. The apartment manager doesn't own the apartments, but runs them on the owner's behalf. The CEO of a public company manages the business on behalf of the owners.

The skills of an NFL athlete are impossible to replicate outside of their body. You and I simply cannot and will never be able to run, catch, and move as well as they can from a football perspective. You and I cannot duplicate the usefulness their physicality brings their Team and League. We cannot swap bodies. Usefulness and control drive income production.

If you do not control the thing that is useful, your ability to make money with it is limited. That's why agents always push to sign exclusive agreements.

In order for you to generate money,

you must control an asset that others find useful.

<u>Question:</u> When somebody can do what you do as well as you, why should anyone pay you really well to do it?

<u>Answer:</u> They don't and they won't. What happens then is competition. The price you can charge has to be reduced as you compete against others that can deliver as you do.

As your usefulness and your ability to control the useful thing decreases, the price that you're able to charge decreases; the reverse is also true, that if either your usefulness or your ability to control it increase, the income that you can make as a result rises (think horse whip manufacturers or Apple computers).

Now in order for you to control the thing that is useful, if you don't already, one of two things must happen: either you create it in some defendable way, OR it's entrusted to you in order to meet goals of the owners.

That's it. Either they are created by you, given to you, or loaned to you to deliver their value on behalf of the owners.

The most common asset we use is our labor. Our employers/customers find our labor (skills, talents) useful and so they pay to secure them.

You always own your labor. That's as far as many of us ever got. But now that we are being led by our Higher Power into a life of healing, usefulness and wealth health we need to expand our thinking.

So for us to generate income we have to be useful and control it. Let's look at these again simply in turn.

For something you create, if it is worthless to others they will not pay for it. If they don't derive value they will not pay you for it.

For something you don't own, in order for you to have control, the owners have to find you useful. This is the common employment, contractor or agent relationship. If you don't provide that value to the owners, they have the right to replace you. It's also that simple.

Either way usefulness to others is the key that unlocks the door. Usefulness is the key for both the haves and the have-nots.

Actions:

Write in your Wealth Journal: List all the physical resources you own or currently have in your control, things like a car, a bike, a strong body, good looks, an education, hustle, whatever.

Write in your Wealth Journal: List people or companies or organizations that could find them useful. Make that list 100 people, companies or organizations.

Write in your Wealth Journal: List in your Journal all your skills and talents that you think you have. Include things that others have told you, even if you don't really believe them. Things like attention to detail, being easy to work with, being a team player, being a leader, your network of people you know or can contact, or your street hustle can all be useful to others.

Write in your Wealth Journal: List people or companies or organizations that could find your skills and talents useful.

Feedback: Bounce the lists you generated off of five people, all of which should know you personally and be more accomplished then you are currently. Ask for their feedback. Bounce this list off of your Flock and ask for their feedback (More about your Flock in the upcoming chapters).

Notes:

Chapter 9: Do your Steps.

Know this:

IF YOU DO NOT DO YOUR STEP WORK, YOU WILL STILL NOT SEE HOW TO BE USEFUL ENOUGH TO OTHERS.

My experience in working with others is that, when I and the guys I work with do not seriously work every day the 12 Steps in our Program of Recovery, while we may be able to do well in a couple of areas, we do not have what it is necessary to excel in all of our 7 areas (the seven are: social, financial, career, physical, family, intellectual, spiritual). We will have gaps. I've seen former addicts and alcoholics be able to maintain maybe three or four areas at a time but not all seven. Powered by Self we are unable to thrive in all seven. For example, it is quite common for us to make serious career moves, and as a result of the time and attention it can sometimes require, gap in the area of our families. Our relationships with our family often become distant or our physical health suffers.

My experience is also that without daily step work, I'm unable to be useful in the ways others really prize and enjoy. I can't really sense what would be useful for them. I'm not humble enough. I'm not open enough. I'm plenty good at being useful in ways I think I should be. Unfortunately, my way neither works for becoming wealthy nor for long term, happy sobriety.

I found I must be useful in ways that others find useful. For example, my mother-in-law needs a couple of items from the pantry to make dinner. Our pantry is one floor beneath the kitchen. When I'm rigorously doing my step work I can pick up on her need and just go down and get them, without her asking. When I'm not, I tend to think how important the thing is I'm doing is, or I focus on how lazy she can be, or I just don't even notice. That's the subtle but very significant difference.

Without rigorous step work, I run out of energy, get mad, get irritable, and can feel resentful. I close to people and my heart hardens. In working with my guys and my sponsor, I know I'm not alone in that. The same things happen to them. It happens to you, even if you're not fully aware. It happens to all of us.

When I'm being selfish, it is also very difficult for me to hear my Higher Power's will for me. Without the step work, I'm not able to reach and sustain a loving, caring, happy integrated life. I feel like I'm always scrambling and falling short. Alcoholics Anonymous talks about the ease gained by the increased connection with our Higher Power as a result of working our steps, pg 88 "We become much more efficient. We do not tire so easily, for we are not burning up energy foolishly as we did when we were trying to arrange life to suit ourselves.

It works—it really does"

Remember page 132: "we think cheerfulness and laughter make for usefulness."

Relentless mental focus on others and how we can help meet their needs is our direction. Working within our code of love and tolerance- for both ourselves and others, supports our efforts to be useful. Seeking to be loving improves our vision, by seeing others better, we are better able to see things that they value and find useful. Our spiritual development as a result of our Program of Action allow us to meet this Good Orderly Direction with cheerfulness and laughter.

The take-a-way is simply and emphatically: Do your Steps!

Actions:

Action: Spend 30 minutes right now on the step you are working. Make a decision, Write on your inventory, pray, ask for help, schedule an amend, make a plan for the day, meditate, become willing, help someone, carry the message, etc.

Call: your sponsees and ask how they are doing.

Action: Prayer and Meditation daily

Call: Call your sponsor, check in and ask what you could do for him or her.

Call: Call five people you don't really know, TODAY, and ask them "What's going on?" Repeat daily

Action: Help someone, doesn't matter who, it doesn't matter how, just do it… NOW.

Notes:

Chapter 10: Your Future is built on what you do Right Now. And only Right Now.

This is both a blessing and a curse.

As you have seen earlier, your future is not determined by the past.

So then what determines your Future?

Your future actually is built from Right Now, this exact moment.

Think it through and you will see it.

Your past provides the context for what's happening right now, but not its substance. For instance, your past decisions have given you the house you live in right now, but not what you can do with it. You could burn it down Right Now and find in the future having to find a new place to live. You could paint a room Right Now and in the future have a different colored room. That's the way to think about this.

The past is done, irrevocable. Done. Done. The future is ALL projection, theory, conjecture, prediction, and inductive reasoning. The NOW is the only place you can take action, it's actually only real place you have any ability to act. The Big Book refers to this concept as "One day at a time." Implicit in that phrase is the understanding that the day we take one at a time is today. The exact truth is that we must take one moment at a time. Science has learned in your diet, for instance, every time you eat, you affect your gut microbes. You feed some and starve others. The same is true for your wealth health. Each transaction matters. The path to being Wealthy is one transaction at a time.

Takeaway- <u>Our future is grown from the RIGHT NOW</u>. Never, ever any other time.

Actions:

Write in your Wealth Journal: Write down what your ideal life would look like.

Write in your Wealth Journal: Write down how the best version of you would behave.

Action: Take a small action, right now, that your ideal you would do.

Write in your Wealth Journal: Immediately following this little ideal you action, do a Gratitude list of 50 items.

Share: Share these lists to your Flock

Write in your Wealth Journal: Imagine what Wealthy action you could take right now to support your Wealth Health for tomorrow.

Write in your Wealth Journal: Figure out how much income you will set aside from each pay to either invest or donate. Set up an automatic system that sets the money in a separate place from your household and personal accounts. Put that amount of money in from your last income receipt. Do this now, even if it hurts a little and makes things tight.

Notes:

Notes:

Chapter 11: Responsibility Circles

The way to think about Responsibility is that it acts like concentric circles. The image begins with you as the center point and radiates outward. The responsibility circles start with you because there is no one on earth you are more responsible for then you. You can do things for yourself that no one else on earth can do for you. For instance, only you can eat at the right times for your body. Only you can get your body to exercise. Only you, and you only. There is no one on earth that is more deserving of your love then you are. Sharon Saltzberg in her amazing book, Lovingkindness, teaches us that.

As you are an addict, that means you are responsible for your Recovery. You are responsible for your choices, for your actions. You are responsible for doing the necessary to maintain and grow your connection with your Higher Power, thereby maintaining and growing your sobriety. No one else on earth is.

As the center point is you, the first circle outward are the people you are in close, intimate relationships with. Common examples of first circle relationships are your partner, your children, and the people you live with. The next circle is friends, colleagues, family. The next circle outward is acquaintances and casual friends and associates. The final circle is strangers. These are, for example, my circles.

You have the most responsibility starting at the center, decreasing as you move outward. The other important quality of this concept is that you must take full care of an inner circle before you take care of an outer one. If you do not, you become unbalanced and out of sequence. It is not appropriate ever to take responsibility for strangers and neglect your kids. Inner first, then outer.

Please be guided by your sponsor and your Higher Power as to the details of who or what are in which circles for you. For instance, some people would put their job in a first or second circle. Putting your job in a first or second circle is totally legitimate, if you understand the overall concept. Please don't be confused and think that because your responsibilities begin with you, all your interest should lie with you. Quoting pg 20 of <u>Alcoholics Anonymous</u>: "Our very lives, as ex-problem drinkers, depend upon our constant thought of others and how we may help meet their needs". Inner first, then outer.

We then over lay the concept of Responsibility Circles with the principles of usefulness, love, caring, kindliness, tolerance, and patience. By overlaying these, we now understand that I am responsible for acting in kindness, love, tolerance, support and patience towards myself first, then my household, then my friends and family, then acquaintances and associates, and then strangers outward. If I am showing patience, tolerance and care towards an acquaintance and not towards my immediate family, I am in violation of this principle and things won't flow.

If I am demonstrating love and tolerance with friends before practicing it for myself, I am in violation of this principle and things also will not flow. I'll feel empty. This is what the Big Book means when the founders say "you can't give away something you don't have." In West Africa they have this great saying for the same wisdom, "Be careful when a naked person offers you a shirt."

Actions:

Write in your Wealth Journal: Write your responsibility circles as you see them. Review them with your Higher Power, your Sponsor and your Flock.

Share: Share them with your partner so that you two can be aligned with what they are for you. Learn what your Partner's are.

Notes:

Chapter 12: Gather the Flock

There is an old saying- "birds of a feather flock together". In my experience there is a deep wisdom to that view. Social science is developing evidence that our performance in life is tightly aligned with the five people we spend the most time with.

Our fellowships communicate the same concept with those tired old clichés: 'If you keep going to a barbershop, eventually you'll get a haircut" and "Beware of people, places and things", and "get in the middle of the herd". For our next concept, we will turn this shared characteristic of ours finally to our advantage, we will gather the Flock. The Flock is a small group of about six people (including you) that meet regularly, no less than once a month to discuss your current circumstances, wealth health and your progress to your goals, dreams and leadings. The flock provides learning, companionship, validation, accountability, acceptance, and clarity, it acts as a sounding board and importantly, a group to celebrate your milestones and achievements with! The key thing is for each of the members of your flock to be more wealthy then you are now.*

These groups have been organized by healthy people for generations. I remember reading about them in Ben Franklin's autobiography. He was a member of a group called the Junto in 18th century Philadelphia. They shared more than just seeking and supporting wealth health, they shared learnings, books, connections, they debated and argued political topics of the day. They provided insurance for each other, a first in the colonies. It was this group that organized the first fire company in America.

Over time as your health improves, you will no longer be the focus of the flock. It may become an opportunity for you to deliver value (altruistic remainders) to the group. Imagine a world that you have five other successful people supporting abundance in your life. Counselling you, guiding you, providing their contacts and help. Imagine not being in this all alone. Imagine people helping you. Now imagine being able to that for them.

We do this together.

———————

If the flock wishes to do the same work for other members, obviously you will meet more frequently and negotiate what works for the team.

Actions:

Write in your Wealth Journal: list 15 people to approach to join your flock. Ask your top 10. They should have the following characteristics: they should be able to commit to meeting regularly for at least for 6months; they should be wealthier than you are now; they each should be people who you respect the lives they lead; they should be able to keep a confidence.

Learning: Have potential Flock members read this ebook so they are familiar with what you are doing and why.

Connection: Make your Flock out of no more than 7 and no less than 4. Meet regularly. Take responsibility to organize and host the meetings. Think about ways getting together will benefit them as well. We are always trying to add value, to contribute altruistically.

Research: Check out Flock Docs (available at www.wealthwoundsworkshop.com). Establish who will keep the Flock's minutes and who guides the group on time.

Network: Join us in the greater Flock,(the larger Flock gathers at www.wealthwoundsworkshop.com) where we share tips and tricks, encouragement and support, daily reminders and monthly activities. Where you can join others in this adventure! We have additional trainings and tools available to you there. All are designed to support you and your Flock at achieving the abundance you are being called for in every aspect of your life.

Notes:

Chapter 13: Budgets and To Do lists

I hated budgets and to-do lists stressed me out. Budgets were too restrictive and took away my freedom. Budgets and working from to do list kills your creativity and your spontaneity, I thought.

How did I solve them and begin using them effectively in life? John Maxwell and Dave Ramsey gave me the key understanding. Dave Ramsey's famous quote is: "A budget is telling your money where to go, instead of wondering where it went."

For me-

A budget is telling my money where to go.

A to do list is telling my time where to go.

Actions:

Action: Do a budget for the balance of this month.

Write in your Wealth Journal: Write down a to-do list. Prioritize it.

Audit: Review every expense last month to see if it is absolutely necessary. If not, do not include it in this month's budget. Try to meet budget for the month. If you budget by day, week or bimonthly, that's fine. Just review performance to it often and make adjustments where necessary. You can't grow usefully without goals and feedback.

Notes:

Chapter 14: Putting it all together

Critical Action 1: <u>Ensure your household spends less then it earns every week.</u>

Critical Action 2: When you make more then you spend: <u>Invest or donate the difference.</u>

Critical Action 3: If, in counsel with your Higher Power, you choose to invest, <u>invest in income producing assets.</u>

It doesn't matter what method you use to accomplish this. There are many strategies and techniques available to you on the internet. We have samples of those that worked for us at <u>www.wealthwoundsworkshop.com</u>. Come check them out.

If you are unable to spend less then you earn, then you are trying to cross a lake in a boat with a hole in it. In that boat are you, your dreams, anyone you're responsible for and all your stuff.

Your boat is leaking and it's only a matter of time before you sink. You are racing against time and praying for calm waters. And you wonder why you feel so tense all the time? Why they call it a rat race? The more you spend greater than your income is the amount of water you take on. Your boat is wounded.

I learned this wealth lesson from my son's preschool teacher. He was teaching us parents about how to help our kindergarteners when they're frustrated. When there is the inevitable fight he taught that, before you start talking about feelings and who did what to whom, you have to stop the fight because, his words: "first, you have to stop the hurting". Hurt people hurt people.

That lesson stuck with me, because the same is true for our wealth wound; we have to plug the leak, we have to consume the minimum we can (even if it is uncomfortable for a little while), make as much as you can (in line with you and your Higher Power's values and priorities) and invest or give away the difference. If you are hurting, the actions to take immediately are twofold: consume less and make more.

When I ask for help with this, this prayer works for me and my sponsees:

"God take from me the desire to live a lifestyle greater than my means, grant me the willingness and strength to consume less and the creativity to earn more by being of greater usefulness to you and my fellows. Amen. Thank you, thank you, thank you"

As you take on less and less water, set aside the money you will use to either invest or give first before anything else. Others have called it "pay yourself first". It works for us. It also works best when it's automatic. Establish an emergency fund (remember your Responsibility Circles) in cash. Others have discussed how large that emergency fund should be, ultimately the decision is yours. We have what has worked for us at www.wealthwoundsworkshop.com. Then we figure out how to live on what remains. Learning to live on what remains is a collection of actions that support our spiritual and altruistic growth. Consume less and make more. Make more by being more useful.

The attractiveness of investing in income producing assets is that eventually you will reach the point where your investments will cover your expenses. When you reach that point, you will no longer need to work for a living. You will be able to spend your full days in whatever it is that your Higher Power would have you do, those things that make your heart sing.

Let me spend a minute to describe what an income producing asset is. An income producing asset is simply one in which generates cash for you. A rental property can be an income producing asset. A CD at a bank can be an income producing asset. Owning a business can be an income producing asset. Owning a stock that generates a dividend can be an income producing asset. Owning an item that people license can be an income producing asset. Owning a story that sells can be an income producing asset. Owning a song that people pay to listen to or play can be an income producing asset. Each of these things are cases where you own or control something that people find useful. Let's look at examples: a rental property can be an income producing asset when your renters pay in excess of your expenses in order to have a place to stay. Here, your renters find shelter useful. A bank finds it useful to pay interest to you to hold your deposit in order to lend or invest it. Look to take advantage of compounding interest whereever possible. Look for situations where you would be paid interest, royalties, dividends or rents.

Rules of Thumb:

You create your financial future with every single transaction. Make each one count.

Your savings are more important than any bill. Remember your Responsibility circles.

Make things automatic. Once established, make them difficult to change.

This is a system of interlocking activities. Every action supports each other. When acting together daily, the activities reinforce each other and rocket you to wealth health. The more you do, the faster you'll go.

Through effort and joy, in every transaction, you create your financial future. You can develop your Wealth Health. You are on the path to becoming Wealthy RIGHT NOW!

You can't usefully grow without feedback.

Consume the absolute minimum, make as much as you can, and if you invest, invest in income producing assets.

Actions:

Write in your Wealthy Journal: Establish goals. Wealthy goals. Goals that are material, clear with clear deadlines. Develop them with your Higher Power. Share them with your Partner.

Write in your Wealthy Journal: Write what your life will look like in 1 year, in 5 years. Ask your Higher Power for its thoughts.

Share: Share these goals with your Flock

Write in your Wealthy Journal: develop a reasonable plan to meet your goals, make it fun. Share the plan with your Flock. Ask for feedback and support. Ask that they hold you accountable.

Write in your Wealthy Journal: Your <u>Better Future Plan</u>. At the beginning, when we decide to save a percentage of our income, we may have to short a bill. Your Better Future plan is your plan for what to do about that bill. Are you going to negotiate a changed payment schedule? Are you going to discontinue the service? What's the plan? What will the consequences be? Review the plan with your Flock. This is a powerful tool and is only to be used sparingly and then only to turn around a financial situation. You will have to meet any obligations you defer in this process. This isn't running from your responsibilities, it is restructuring them. If you can't save, you are sinking. You must reduce your spending. We must stop the hurting first. I have a sample copy of a <u>Better Future Plan</u> for you at <u>www.wealthwoundsworkshop.com</u>, it's in the section FlockDocs.

Review: Review your performance against your Budget. Share the results with your Flock.

Notes:

In closing,

I loved sharing what I've learned over these last years with you. Come check out our community of people getting wealthy at the site www.wealthwoundsworkshop.com. It's where you can find additional resources like our recommendations for budgets, Flock Docs and Your Wealth Journal. There is also where you can find the larger Flock, all of us walking together in this process and each committed to supporting you in your healing process.

Let me leave you with two of my favorite passages from the Big Book of Alcoholics Anonymous:

Those of us who have spent much time in the world of spiritual make-believe have eventually seen the childishness of it. This dream world has been replaced by a great sense of purpose, accompanied by a growing consciousness of the power of God in our lives. We have come to believe He would like us to keep our heads in the clouds with Him, but that our feet ought to be firmly planted on earth. That is where our fellow travelers are, and that is where our work must be done. These are the realities for us. We have found nothing incompatible between a powerful spiritual experience and a life of sane and happy usefulness.

Alcoholics Anonymous Pg 130.

Our book is meant to be suggestive only. We realize we know only a little. God will constantly disclose more to you and to us. Ask him in your morning meditation what you can do each day for the man who is still sick. The answers will come, if your own house is in order. But obviously you cannot transmit something you haven't got. See to it that your relationship with him is right, and great events will come to pass for you and countless others. This is the Great Fact for us.

Abandon yourself to God as you understand God. Admit your faults to him and to your fellows. Clear away the wreckage of your past. Give freely of what you find and join us. We shall be with you in the Fellowship of the Spirit, and you will surely meet some of us as you trudge the road of Happy Destiny.

May God bless you and keep you-until then.

Alcoholics Anonymous, Pg164

Action Summaries

Actions:

- **Write in your Wealth Journal**: How has your shying away from facing your relationship to money affected you?
- **Write in your Wealth Journal**: What could your life look like if you became wealth healthy today?

Actions:

- **Write in your Wealth Journal:** List your regrets- Describe what happened, who it hurt, it what was your part in the regrets?
- **Share:** Share your regrets list with another person.
- **Write in your Wealth Journal:** Write about what it will feel like to make these same regrets again? Because very similar regrets will happen again if you do not change your behavior.
- **Write in your Wealth Journal:** Name what was the best action you did today for your Wealth Health? What was it and how did it make you feel?
- **Say Thanks:** Say thank you to your Higher Power for the power to have done the best thing you did that day for your Wealth Health.
- **Action:** Forgiveness Practice

    First- Create a list of people you're mad at and/or have harmed you in some way.

    Second- Start at the top of the list and write about your part in the situation, what would you have done differently if you could do it over.

Third- Reflect on the mistakes you have made

Fourth- Understand that these people are the same as you; they are simply souls trying to be happy just like you. They're doing the best they can. And just like you, sometimes they misunderstand how to be happy.

Fifth- Begin with yourself. Pray this Prayer for 90 days in a row: *"God thank you for the Grace to have made it this far. I've been doing the best I could with what I've known. Please show me every day the way of patience, tolerance, kindliness and love for myself and for others. Please help me lay down those actions and feelings that no longer serve who you would have me be. Please show me every day who you would have me be and give me the strength to do your Will. Amen"*

Sixth- Pray that everything good that you want for yourself comes to the person you are working on forgiving. As your heart softens, move on to the next person. Do this daily.

- **Say Thanks:** At night, think about your favorite thing that happened that day and give thanks to your Higher Power for its happening.

Actions:

- **Write in your Wealth Health Journal-**
    - What is your story?
    - What ideas of wealth were around you as a kid?
    - What was your parent's relationship to money?
    - What was your close family's relationships to money?
    - What was your neighborhood like?
    - Did someone close to you make a lot of money? How were they treated?
    - Was your family financially healthy or did they do the best they knew how?
    - What stories were told about wealth and money?

Actions:

- **Write in your Wealth Journal:** Answer these questions in your journal:
    - What would you do if you had unlimited dollars?
    - What in this world would you experience?
    - Who would you take with you?
    - What would you do with your time?
    - What would you do for your kids? For your partner?
    - What would you do for your family? For your friends?
    - Who would you help? Why?
    - What would you make right?
    - What causes would you support?
    - What would you give to charity?
    - What would you have done if you had had unlimited dollars five years ago? Ten years?
    - Where would you and your family be right now? What would you have done already?
    - What would it feel like to be Wealth Healthy right now?

Actions:

- **Write in your Wealth Journal:** A Hundred- A Hundred is a 100 item gratitude list.
  - It's to be done in the following format:
    Thank you, thank you, thank you from the bottom of my heart for (the thing you are grateful for) because (reason you are grateful).

For example: Thank you, thank you, thank you for my son is healthy, because we would be so scared if he was sick and I don't ever want him to suffer.

Actions:

- **Question:** Ask your friends for ideas on how you can be more useful to your employers, your clients, your fans, your colleagues or your customers. Write their answers in your Wealth Journal. Your goal is to get a list of 50 separate ideas in your journal. If anyone of your friends repeats an idea, really try to figure out how you could make it happen.
- **Write in your Wealth Journal:** List one thing for each of ten different people that you could do for them that they would find useful or valuable. Things that they would like and appreciate.
- **Write in your Wealth Journal:** Write about how you could make each of those actions better for each of the 10 people. Possible examples are: by doing the action right now, doing it in a friendlier manner, or by reducing their costs.
- **Action:** Do one of those actions <u>right now</u> for one of those 10 people.
- **Action and List:** Go through your list of friends on Facebook and list one thing for each friend that would help them feel better, meet a goal, or meet someone that could be a useful connection for

them. If you don't know what would help them, ask them now.

- **Action:** Do one useful thing each day for each of your friends, including your Facebook friends, starting first with those that you see most.
- **Action:** Each day do three anonymous good, useful, kind and compassionate deeds. Don't break the chain.
- **Action:** Count the number of nice, kind, helpful, useful things you do for somebody else that you didn't feel like doing. Share that number with a friend or a group of friends every day.
- **Action:** Tell a friend about the benefits you've experienced from these practices.
- **Action:** Tell a friend about information that you've found useful, which would be useful to them.
- **Action:** Tell a friend about this book and where they could buy it, tell them about the idea of Altruistic Remainders.
- **Action:** Make an introduction between two of your contacts that would be useful to at least one of them. Make it warm and inviting.

Actions:

- **Write in your Journal:** Brainstorm how you could add value, even very simple value to those around you at work. Or school. Or in the car, all those place you find yourself. Try a couple of them this week.

Actions:

- **Write in your Wealth Journal:** List all the physical resources you own or currently have in your control on the behalf of others, things like a car, a bike, a strong body, good looks, an education, hustle, whatever.
- **Write in your Wealth Journal:** List people or companies or organizations that could find them useful. Make that list 100 people, companies or organizations.
- **Write in your Wealth Journal:** List in your Journal all your skills and talents that you think you have. Include things that others have told you, even if you don't really believe them. Things like attention to detail, your network of people you know or can contact, or your street hustle.
- **Write in your Wealth Journal:** List people or companies or organizations that could find your skills and talents useful.
- **Feedback:** Bounce the lists you generated off of five people, all of which should know you personally and be more accomplished then you are currently. Ask for their feedback. Bounce this list off of your Flock and ask for their feedback.

Actions:

- **Action:** Spend 30 minutes right now on the step you are working. Make a decision, Write on your inventory, pray, ask for help, schedule an amend, make a plan for the day, meditate, help someone, etc.
- **Call:** your sponsees and ask how they are doing.
- **Action: Prayer and Meditation daily**
- **Call**: Call your sponsor, check in and ask what you could do for him or her.
- **Call**: Call five people you don't really know, TODAY, and ask them "What's going on?" Repeat daily
- **Action**: Help someone, doesn't matter who, it doesn't matter how, just do it… NOW.

Actions:

- **Write in your Wealth Journal:** Write down what your ideal life would look like.
- **Write in your Wealth Journal:** Write down how the best version of you would behave.
- **Action:** Take a small action, right now, that your ideal you would do.
- **Write in your Wealth Journal:** Immediately following this little ideal you action, do a Gratitude list of 50 items.
- **Share:** Share these lists to your Flock
- **Write in your Wealth Journal:** Imagine what Wealthy action you could take right now to support your Wealth Health for tomorrow.
- **Write in your Wealth Journal**: Figure out how much income you will set aside from each pay to either invest or donate. Set up an automatic system that sets the money in a separate place from your household and personal accounts. Put that amount of money in from your last income receipt. Do this now, even if it hurts a little and makes things tight.

Actions:

- **Write in your Wealth Journal:** Write your responsibility circles as you see them. Review them with your Higher Power, your Sponsor and your Flock.
- **Share:** Share them with your partner so that you two can be aligned with what they are for you.

Actions:

- **Write in your Wealth Journal:** list 15 people to approach to join your flock. Ask your top 10. They should have the following characteristics: they should be able to commit to meeting regularly for at least for 6months; they should be wealthier than you are now; they each should be people who you respect the lives they lead; they should be able to keep a confidence.

- **Learning:** Have potential Flock members read this ebook so they are familiar with what you are doing and why.

- **Connection:** Make your Flock out of no more than 7 and no less than 4. Meet regularly. Take responsibility to organize and host the meetings. Think about ways getting together will benefit them as well. We are always trying to add value, to contribute altruistically.

- **Research:** Check out The Flock Doc's. Establish who will keep the Flock's minutes and who guides the group on time.

- **Network:** Join us in the greater Flock, where we share tips and tricks, encouragement and support, daily reminders and monthly activities. Where you can join others in this adventure! We have additional trainings and tools available to you there. All are designed to support you and your Flock at achieving the abundance you are being called for in every aspect of your life.

- **Network:** Sign up now at www.healingwealthwounds.com so you can continue to be supported as become wealthy for you, your family, your friends and the causes and issues you care about!

Actions:

- **Action:** Do a budget for the balance of this month.
- **Write in your Wealth Journal:** Write down a to-do list. Prioritize it.
- **Audit:** Review every expense last month to see if it is absolutely necessary. If not, do not include it in this month's budget. Try to meet budget for the month. If you budget by day, week or bimonthly, that's fine. Just review performance to it often and make adjustments where necessary. You can't grow usefully without goals and feedback.

Actions:

- **Write in your Wealthy Journal:** Establish goals. Wealthy goals. Goals that are material, clear with clear deadlines. Develop them with your Higher Power. Share them with your Partner.
- **Write in your Wealthy Journal:** Write what your life will look like in 1 year, in 5 years. Ask your Higher Power for its thoughts.
- **Share:** Share these goals with your Flock
- **Write in your Wealthy Journal:** develop a reasonable plan to meet your goals, make it fun. Share the plan with your Flock. Ask for feedback and support. Ask that they hold you accountable.
- **Review:** Review your purchases against your Budget. Share the results with your Flock.

Wealth Wounds Workbook

I am so excited that you are taking this step to heal your Wealth Wounds! We'll be with you as we walk this road together.

The workbook will allow you to really understand the core issues that have held you back in the past, start working through them and accelerate your growth and progress.

You will also find the basic, no BS, rocksolid budget and to-do framework allowing you to have laser focus on these building blocks for your new wealthy life..

SIGN UP HERE and you will automatically receive a FREE PDF copy of the Wealth Wounds Companion Workbook. If you're working from a hard copy, just go to the link http://mad.ly/signups/125811/join and sign up. I will make sure you get your copy.

This list is private, not sold or rented and never shared with anyone. I may occasionally email you updates about Wealth Wounds products, tips, tricks and more information. You can opt-out at any time!

www.ingramcontent.com/pod-product-compliance
Lightning Source LLC
Chambersburg PA
CBHW051707170526
45167CB00002B/567